Introduction

Fantasy is one of the most exciting genres to draw for. There are no rules and anything is possible. You can stick to the established conventions already out there, or let your imagination run wild.

Fantasy worlds aren't just populated with sensational monsters. They're full of equally fantastical races of people. Heroes, villains, and the everyday person can be anything and everything you can imagine.

Your fantasy world can be a realm of medieval mayhem, wayward peasants fighting evil sorcerers to save that elusive princess. Maybe you don't want to stick to a preestablished convention; your fantasy world could be a mix of modern technology and magical creatures. Maybe your world is full of bits and pieces of several different myths, combined with something uniquely your own.

With all the variety in characters, costumes, monsters and environments, fantasy is a genre that can keep you interested with enough new and exciting things to imagine and create for a lifetime!

Table of Contents

HOW TO USE THIS BOOK	3
BASIC SHAPES	4
SHADING AND 3-D EFFECTS	5
PENCILING AND INKING	6
COLORING	7
HUMAN BODY	8
FAIRY	10
ORC	14
GOBLIN	18
DWARF	22
CENTAUR	26
SPRITE	30

How to Use This Book

Fantasy creatures, by their very nature, have no firm blueprints. In made-up worlds, rules are made to be broken. However, the creatures all share some similar characteristics. Anatomy must be functional. By studying each piece of the anatomy and understanding how it works, you'll learn to build your own characters.

This book consists of several easy-to-follow step-by-step demonstrations. Each new step of each demonstration is denoted in red. Following along with the demonstrations will help you draw several different, truly fantastic creatures. Look out for Dolosus, your fierce dragon guide, and Harold, his incompetent minion, along the way, too. They show up here and there to provide helpful tips and tricks to ease your passage.

Don't be discouraged if your first efforts don't look exactly as you planned. Everything comes with practice. The more you draw, the better you'll get. Through sheer repetition, your drawings will improve and your own personal style will emerge. If each drawing you make looks a little bit better than the previous one, you're getting somewhere.

So sharpen your pencils, find your softest eraser, prepare your trusty inking pen, and let's go!

>1<

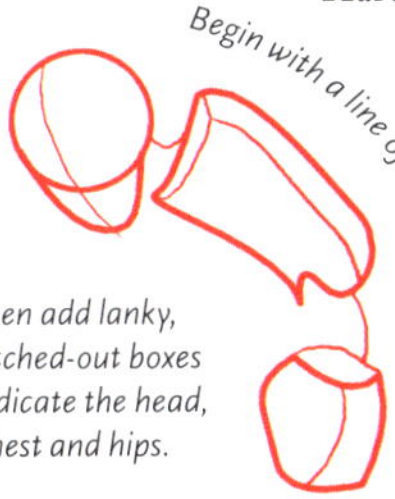

Begin with a line of motion.

Then add lanky, stretched-out boxes to indicate the head, chest and hips.

>2<

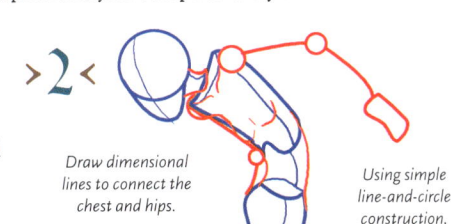

Draw dimensional lines to connect the chest and hips.

Using simple line-and-circle construction, sketch in the arms.

To help you navigate this wonder of a book, adorable mascots have been employed to show you the way.

So that the awesomeness that is Dolosus doesn't overwhelm you, we've hired another mascot to help be underwhelming.

Wait... I only work alone.

Hello!

BASIC SHAPES

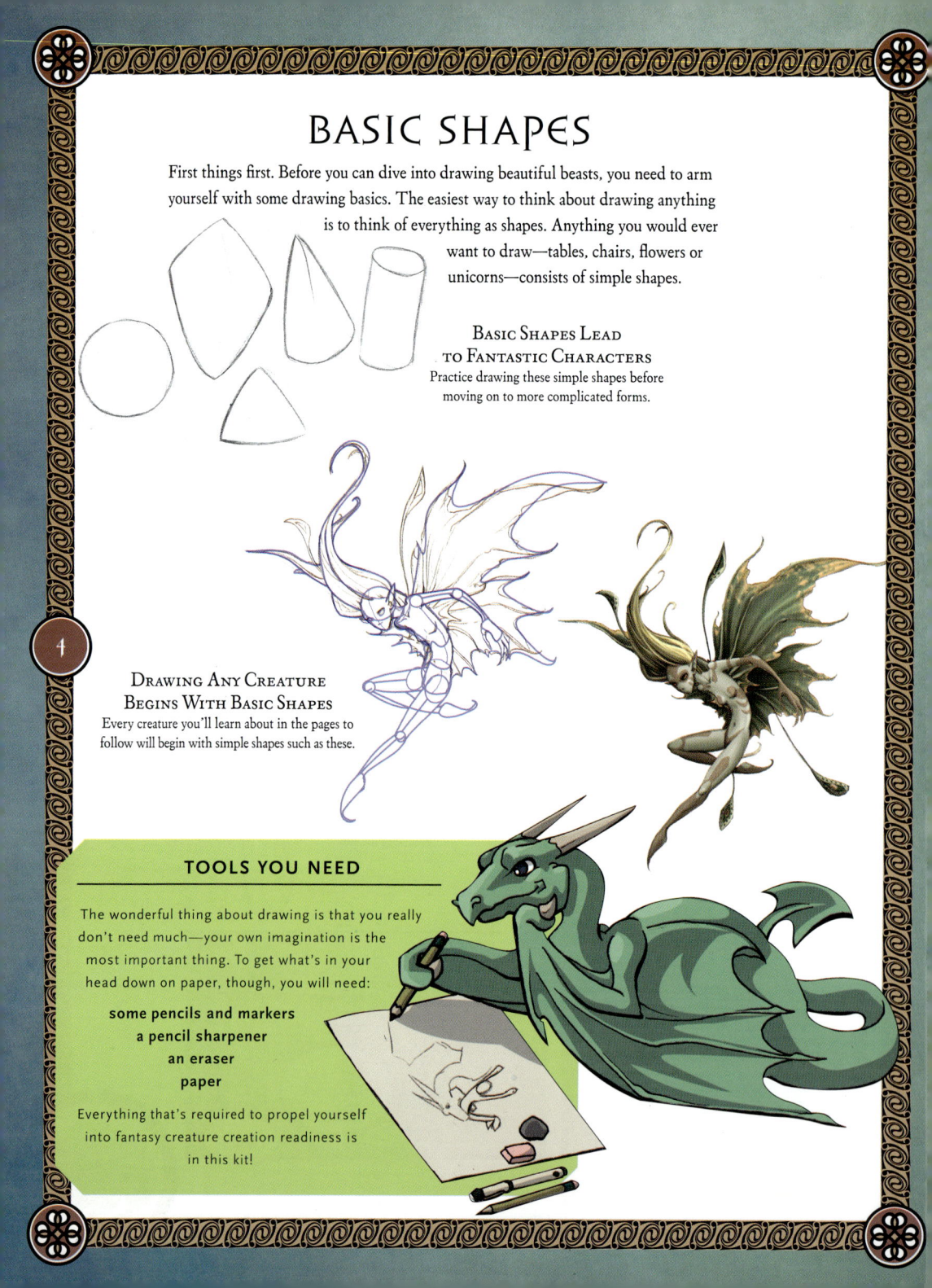

First things first. Before you can dive into drawing beautiful beasts, you need to arm yourself with some drawing basics. The easiest way to think about drawing anything is to think of everything as shapes. Anything you would ever want to draw—tables, chairs, flowers or unicorns—consists of simple shapes.

Basic Shapes Lead to Fantastic Characters
Practice drawing these simple shapes before moving on to more complicated forms.

Drawing Any Creature Begins With Basic Shapes
Every creature you'll learn about in the pages to follow will begin with simple shapes such as these.

TOOLS YOU NEED

The wonderful thing about drawing is that you really don't need much—your own imagination is the most important thing. To get what's in your head down on paper, though, you will need:

**some pencils and markers
a pencil sharpener
an eraser
paper**

Everything that's required to propel yourself into fantasy creature creation readiness is in this kit!

SHADING AND 3-D EFFECTS

Fantasy characters appear more realistic when you draw them to look three-dimensional. It isn't as hard as it sounds. You just have to pay attention to darks and lights and how they affect your creature.

Consider first where the light is coming from. This is called the light source. Where the light source hits your dragon or other object is the lightest spot, called the highlight. The rest of your creature will likely be in some stage of shadow. As you develop your skills at shading the shadow areas, your creatures will begin to take on new life.

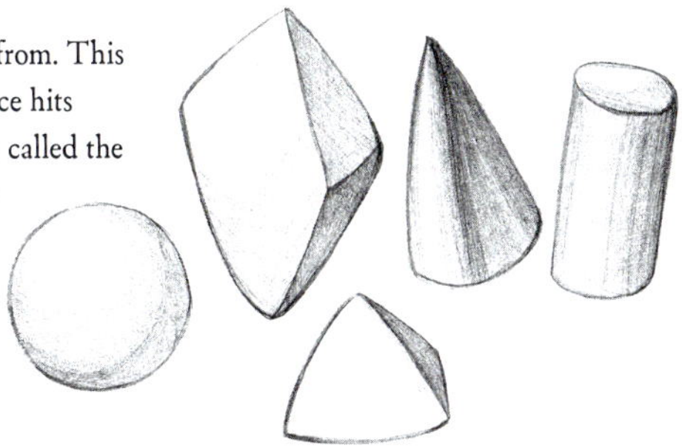

Practice on Simple Shapes

Polygons (shapes with three or more sides) will often have one side facing the light source. This side will be considerably lighter than those angled in a different direction. Sides that are completely cut off from the light will be very dark, giving you a harsh edge.

With round objects there is no clear definition of where things get cut off from direct light. The answer to this problem is fairly simple: Because there's a gradual cutoff from the light, you will have gradual shadow with no harsh edges. Figure out where your light is hitting directly, and as things move farther away from that point of light, they should get darker.

Simple Pencil Techniques for Shading

1. Scribble—Swirl your pencil in overlapping circles. 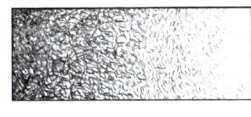
2. Stipple—Place dots close together or far apart. 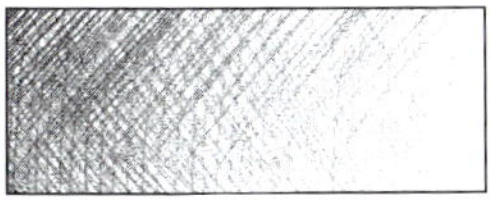
3. Crosshatching—Lay hatch marks, one over the other. 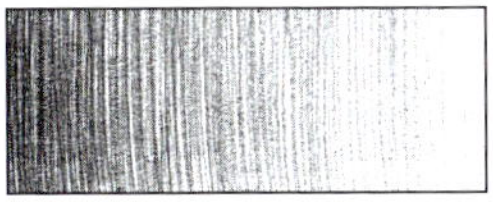
4. Hatching—Place short lines close together or far apart.

BE AWARE OF THE LIGHT SOURCE

As cool as fantasy characters are, they remain solid, tangible objects that follow the same laws as everything else when it comes to light source. Lighting that comes from a single direction will yield highlights on the surfaces that it hits, and shadows on the areas blocked off from the rays.

PENCILING AND INKING

You may want to keep your pencil lines very soft and natural looking, and just paint right on top of them, so in the end you have no linework at all. Inking your drawing is an equally interesting approach. An inked drawing makes your character very crisp and clean, and will make coloring much easier later on, as you've already begun defining your character. Inking also makes line cleanup easy. Just draw all your construction lines in pencil, then do your finals in ink. When you're finished, go back in with an eraser and rub it over the entire drawing, leaving only the final ink lines behind.

A ballpoint pen will give you a finer, more varied ink line than markers, but watch for smudging! Some ballpoint pens leave unequal amounts of ink in a line, causing much grief later on. Markers are not always the best solution either because they are very susceptible to bleeding. Many art stores carry disposable technical pens that are ideal for starting out with inks. They are fairly cheap, come in different colors and are easy to use.

Pencil
Pencil lines are light and easy to cover with ink or paint. If you would like your pencil lines to show, you can use a mechanical pencil to tighten up your linework. Then, you can take it into your favorite computer program and color it. If you leave your pencil drawing as is, you can easily shade it with a variety of soft and hard leads.

Ballpoint Pen
Ballpoint is nice because it's possible to do very light lines and shade as well. You can achieve delicate linework that is difficult to achieve with other inking tools. Compared to a pencil, though, erasing is difficult.

Technical Pen
Technical pens create very thin, sharp lines, perfect for comic books. Shading with liquid ink involves a series of line widths, hatching, stippling and cross-hatching. It's not possible to get a series of grays with the ink itself, because it will always come out black. Use a Micron pen if you want a clean unshaded drawing, or a drawing that's shaded using linework with a lot of character.

Brushpen
A brushpen allows you to create thick and thin organic lines. Your lines will never be as delicate or exact as those done with ballpoint or technical pens, but you can achieve a lot of character and inking speed with a brushpen.

COLORING

You can take several different approaches to color as you plan out your characters. Color combined with lighting sets the mood for any image. Desaturated colors and earth tones will give you a soft, natural-looking image. If you place some vibrant colors against mostly neutral colors, those vibrant colors will seem very bright, almost glowing. Vibrant colors set against a neonlike setting won't stand out as much. If you want your characters to really pop out from the page, color them just a touch more boldly than the background. Making good color choices will make your characters look believable. For instance, orange with pink and green polka dots may not be a great choice for a vampire's skin.

THE COLOR WHEEL

The color wheel is a great tool to help you plan out your character's color scheme. The primary colors are red, yellow and blue. The secondary colors are orange, green and purple. Complementary colors sit across from each other and analogous colors sit next to each other.

Color Chaos

You can paint your character with a rainbow of colors, picking out the ones you like best and seeing where it goes. You don't have to follow a specific coloring strategy if you don't want to, but if you find your image isn't coming together how you would like, thinking ahead and using a coloring strategy may be beneficial.

Analogous Colors

Analogous colors, or families of colors, are colors that are next to each other on the color wheel. In this case, shades of red-orange, orange, and yellow-orange were used to color the image with some purple to make it pop. This allows for more variety of color than a monochromatic image while still having your colors feel largely the same.

Monochromatic Colors

A simple way to bring an image together is to use monochromatic colors. That is, you use varying shades and intensities of the same color. The colors will look like they belong together, because they are all the same hue. You can bring in little bits of other colors here and there for variety.

Desaturated Colors

Not all colors need to be bright. Just because your character's hair is pink doesn't mean it needs to be the pinkest pink available. Toning down all your colors will give you a more natural image and may help avoid rainbow chaos.

HUMAN BODY

Start With Simple Shapes
Before investing a lot of time in a pose, sketch out an extremely loose framework. Use 3-D boxes to represent the head, chest and hips to show the direction a figure is facing and the movement it's making. If your simple line-and-circle sketch isn't okay, you'll have only spent like one minute drawing out the stick and box figure. Erase that sucker and try again.

HUMAN BODY (FEMALE FOCUS)

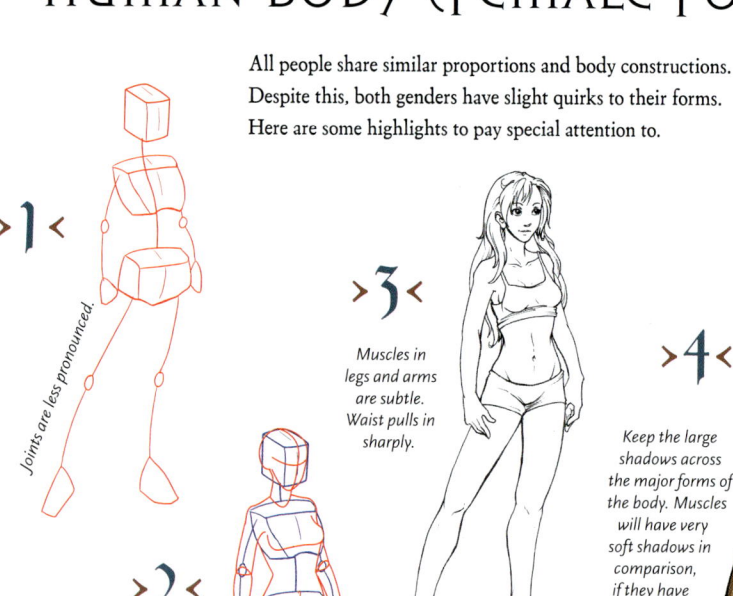

All people share similar proportions and body constructions. Despite this, both genders have slight quirks to their forms. Here are some highlights to pay special attention to.

>1<

Joints are less pronounced.

>2<

Breasts sit above the rib cage. Hips pull outward from the waist, and are generally larger and more pronounced than in males.

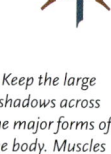

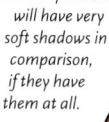

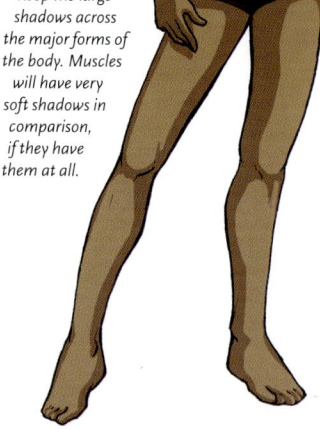

>3<

Muscles in legs and arms are subtle. Waist pulls in sharply.

>4<

Keep the large shadows across the major forms of the body. Muscles will have very soft shadows in comparison, if they have them at all.

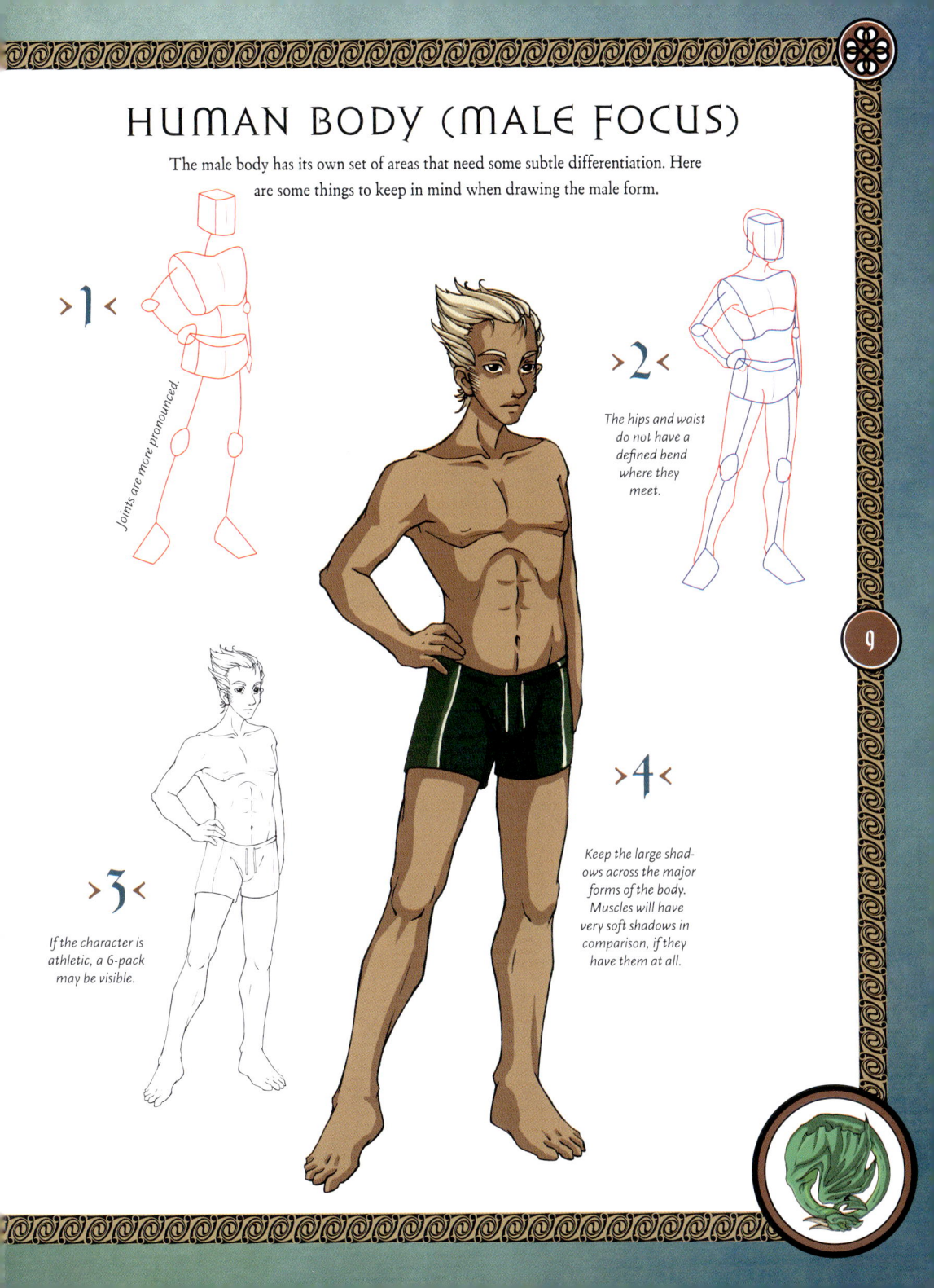

HUMAN BODY (MALE FOCUS)

The male body has its own set of areas that need some subtle differentiation. Here are some things to keep in mind when drawing the male form.

>1<

Joints are more pronounced.

>2<

The hips and waist do not have a defined bend where they meet.

>3<

If the character is athletic, a 6-pack may be visible.

>4<

Keep the large shadows across the major forms of the body. Muscles will have very soft shadows in comparison, if they have them at all.

Fairy

Fairies have always been an important part in European mythology and fairy tales. The fairies of myth and legend were both mischievous and benevolent. The fairies that we draw today may be the same, tricky creatures or a reflection of our world today. Urban fairies, anyone?

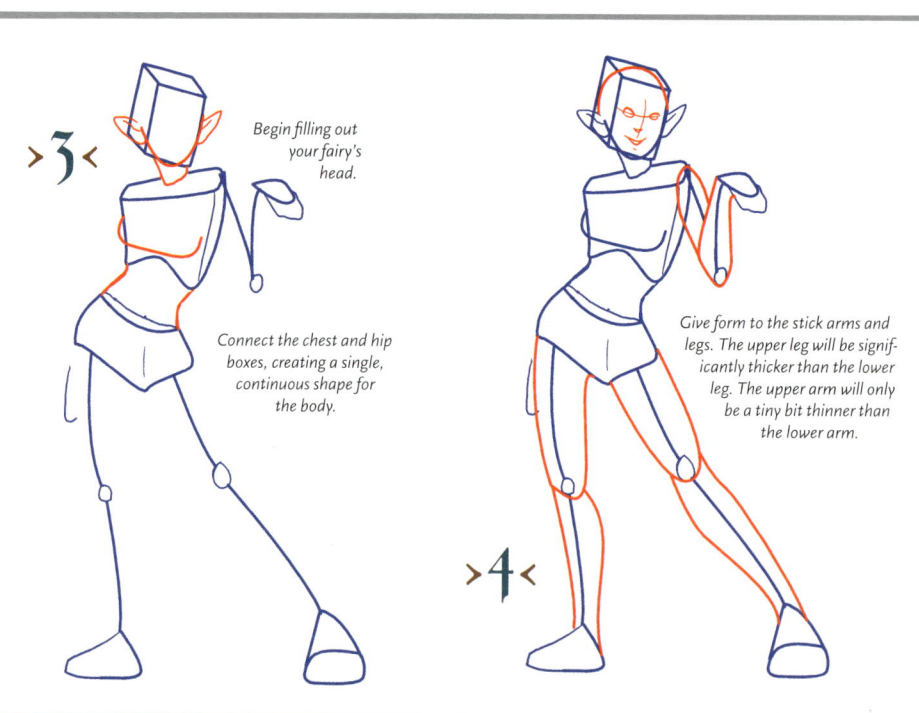

I—I think this is a bad idea. Are you sure this will help people learn to draw?

Who can say for certain, but have faith, my minion!

The work we do within these comics is important, nay, invaluable!

Somehow I doubt this has any value.

Trust me, people will never forget what we do here today.

That's what I'm afraid of.

> 3 <

Begin filling out your fairy's head.

Connect the chest and hip boxes, creating a single, continuous shape for the body.

> 4 <

Give form to the stick arms and legs. The upper leg will be significantly thicker than the lower leg. The upper arm will only be a tiny bit thinner than the lower arm.

> 1 <

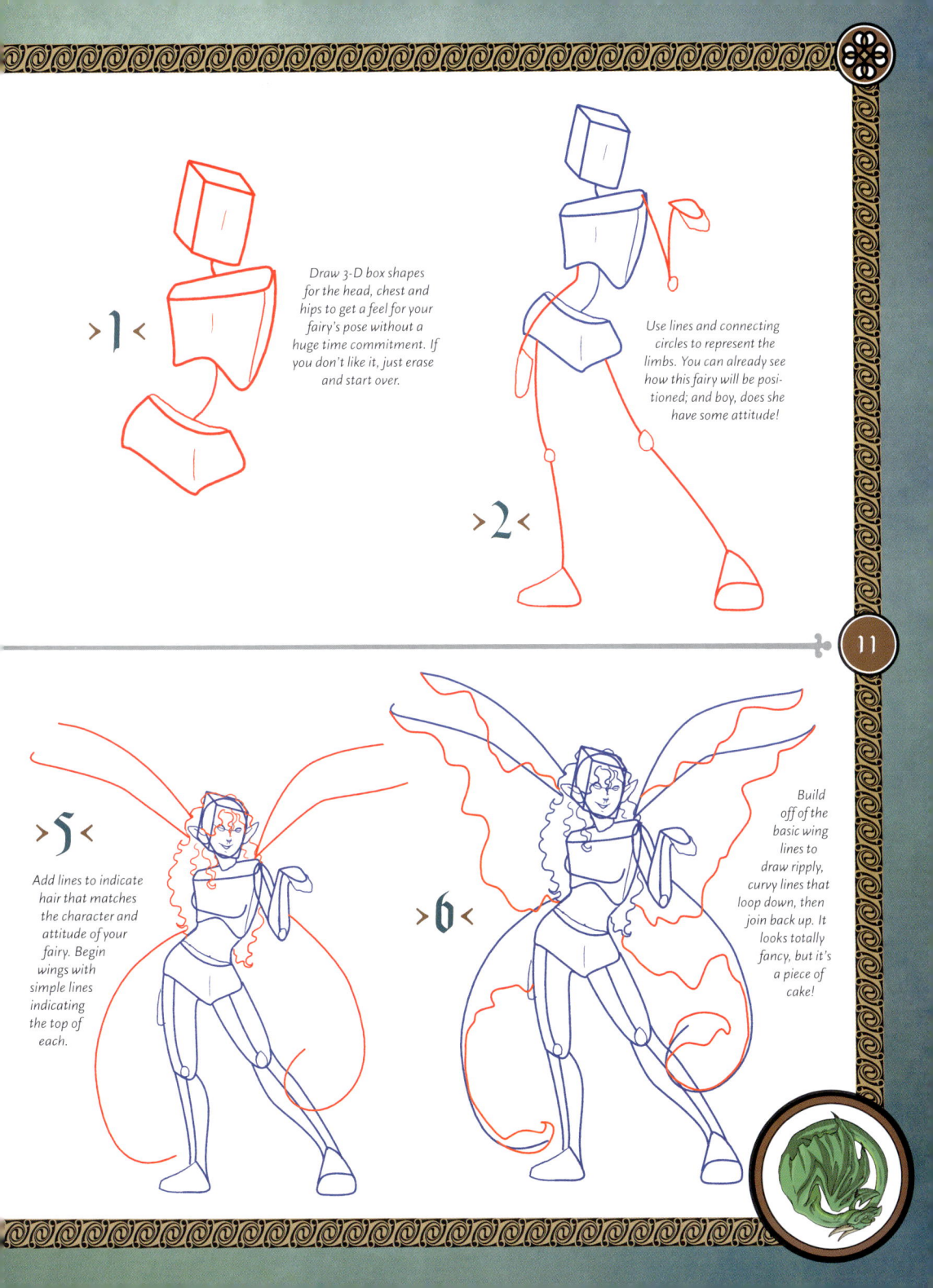

Draw 3-D box shapes for the head, chest and hips to get a feel for your fairy's pose without a huge time commitment. If you don't like it, just erase and start over.

> 2 <

Use lines and connecting circles to represent the limbs. You can already see how this fairy will be positioned; and boy, does she have some attitude!

> 5 <

Add lines to indicate hair that matches the character and attitude of your fairy. Begin wings with simple lines indicating the top of each.

> 6 <

Build off of the basic wing lines to draw ripply, curvy lines that loop down, then join back up. It looks totally fancy, but it's a piece of cake!

> 7 <

Begin adding costuming to your figure. Garments that are pulled tightly across the body will conform to its shape. Cloth that is unbound will hang loose and be pulled mainly by gravity. The costuming possibilities are limitless. You could have a warrior fairy, a pirate fairy, a river fairy, a vine-covered fairy, a noble fairy. . . anything! Plan out what you would like to do beforehand so you have a good strategy.

> 8 <

Erase any stray construction lines, and give it a good look over. Is she totally ready for color? Of course she is!

Choose colors that go with your fairy's personality. Got a mysterious fairy? Blacks and purples might be right up your alley. Sweet and innocent? Maybe some soft blues or pinks. This fairy is all about attitude, so I chose a nice bright scarlet.

> 9 <

> 10 <

Finish off your fairy with an environment or decorative background. Tah-dah! Instant awesome! (Okay, it's not instant, but "instant awesome" sounds way cooler than "well-thought-out-art-piece awesome.")

The Passion of Scarlet

Orc

The orc was a creature originally developed by J.R.R. Tolkien. Today, orcs have become a very common, but very important part of modern fantasy. You'll see orcs in modern fantasy novels, role-playing games and video games. They're often described as brutish, with large tusks, brows and chests. They're dirty more often than not, and come in earthy colors ranging from gray to brown to green.

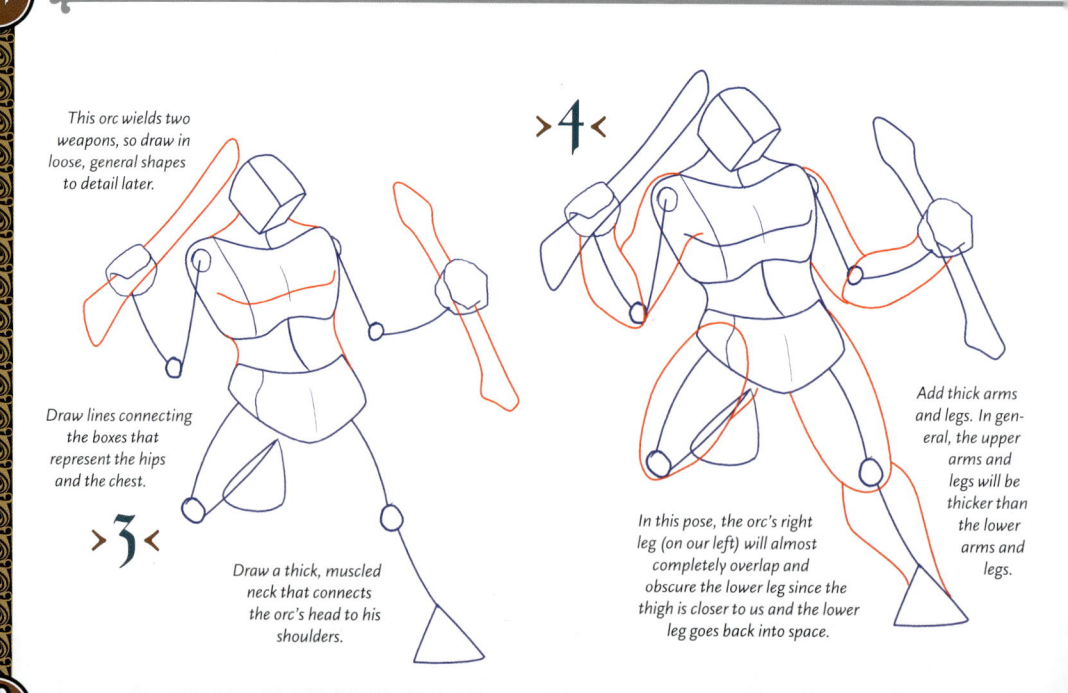

Art doesn't always come easy. Some images will give you trouble over and over.

It happens to everyone. Take a break and try drawing something else. Come back to the problem image later.

Don't stress.

And don't get angry.

Because carbon just isn't that much fun to look at later on.

>3<

This orc wields two weapons, so draw in loose, general shapes to detail later.

Draw lines connecting the boxes that represent the hips and the chest.

Draw a thick, muscled neck that connects the orc's head to his shoulders.

>4<

Add thick arms and legs. In general, the upper arms and legs will be thicker than the lower arms and legs.

In this pose, the orc's right leg (on our left) will almost completely overlap and obscure the lower leg since the thigh is closer to us and the lower leg goes back into space.

> 1 <

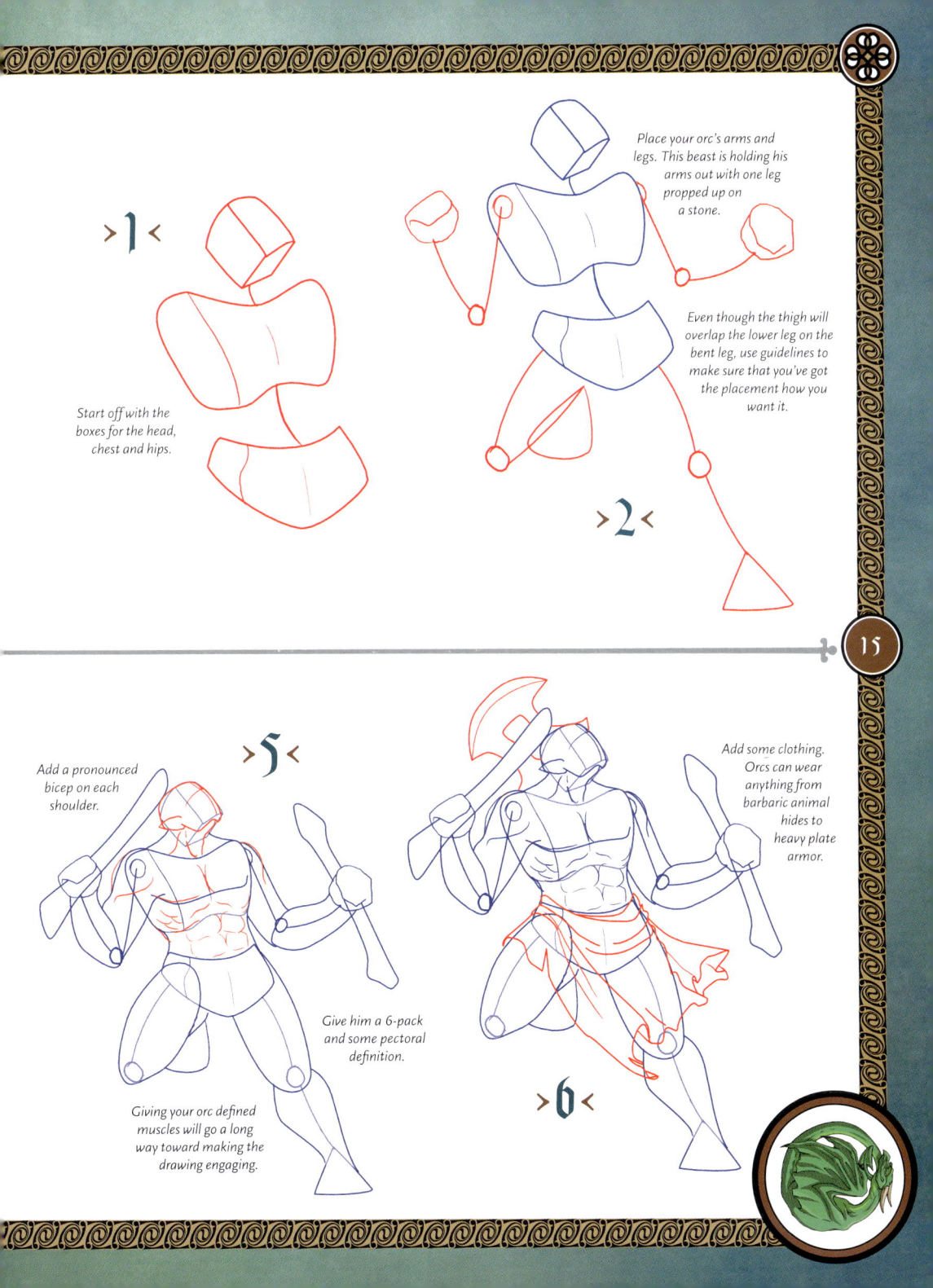

Start off with the boxes for the head, chest and hips.

Place your orc's arms and legs. This beast is holding his arms out with one leg propped up on a stone.

Even though the thigh will overlap the lower leg on the bent leg, use guidelines to make sure that you've got the placement how you want it.

> 2 <

> 5 <

Add a pronounced bicep on each shoulder.

Give him a 6-pack and some pectoral definition.

Giving your orc defined muscles will go a long way toward making the drawing engaging.

Add some clothing. Orcs can wear anything from barbaric animal hides to heavy plate armor.

> 6 <

>7<

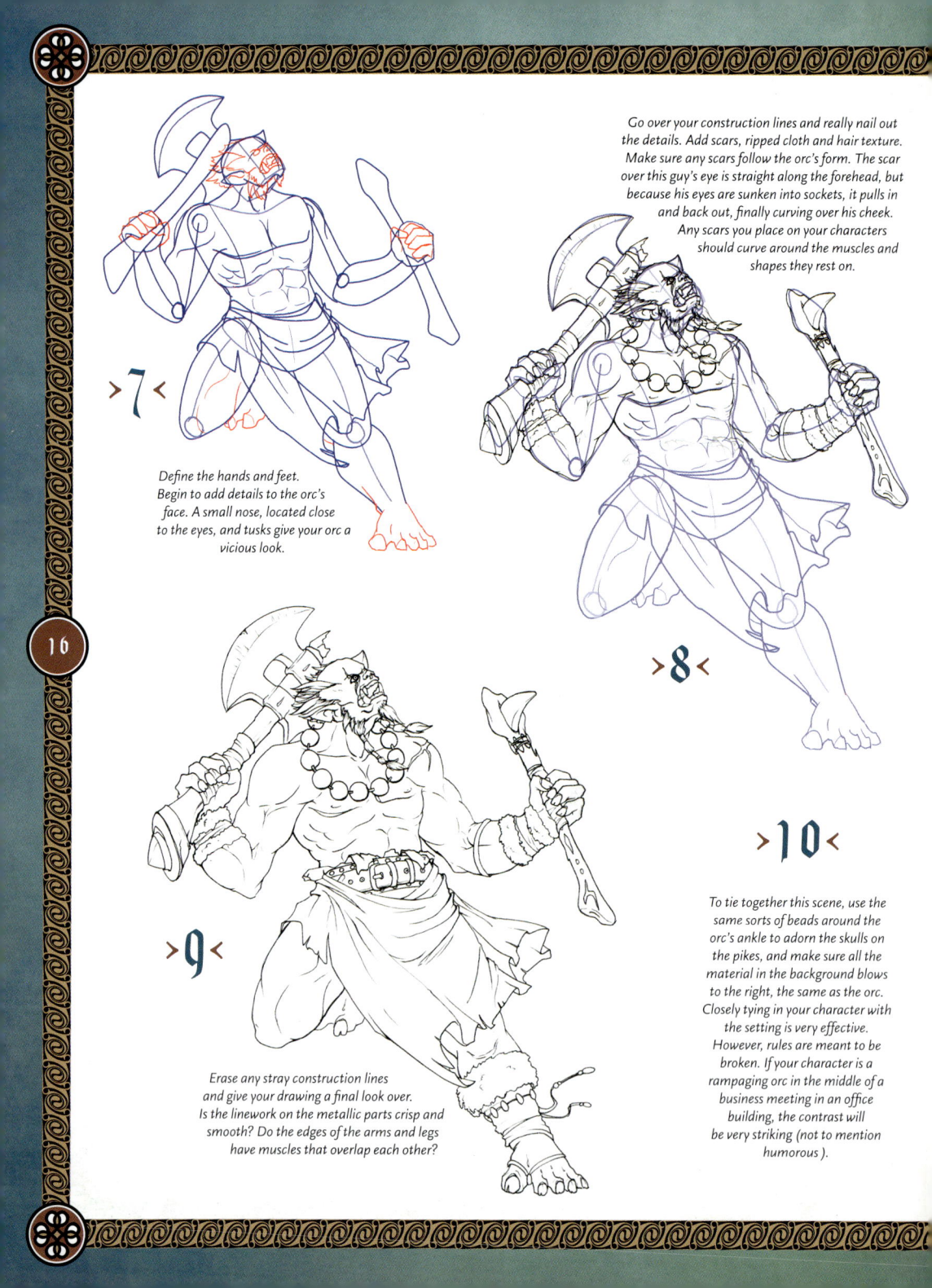

Define the hands and feet. Begin to add details to the orc's face. A small nose, located close to the eyes, and tusks give your orc a vicious look.

>8<

Go over your construction lines and really nail out the details. Add scars, ripped cloth and hair texture. Make sure any scars follow the orc's form. The scar over this guy's eye is straight along the forehead, but because his eyes are sunken into sockets, it pulls in and back out, finally curving over his cheek. Any scars you place on your characters should curve around the muscles and shapes they rest on.

>9<

Erase any stray construction lines and give your drawing a final look over. Is the linework on the metallic parts crisp and smooth? Do the edges of the arms and legs have muscles that overlap each other?

>10<

To tie together this scene, use the same sorts of beads around the orc's ankle to adorn the skulls on the pikes, and make sure all the material in the background blows to the right, the same as the orc. Closely tying in your character with the setting is very effective. However, rules are meant to be broken. If your character is a rampaging orc in the middle of a business meeting in an office building, the contrast will be very striking (not to mention humorous).

17

Goblin

Goblins are mischievous, sometimes wicked little fairies that enjoy playing tricks on unsuspecting people. Once you draw a goblin, watch your desk carefully. If your art supplies go missing, you'll know who to blame.

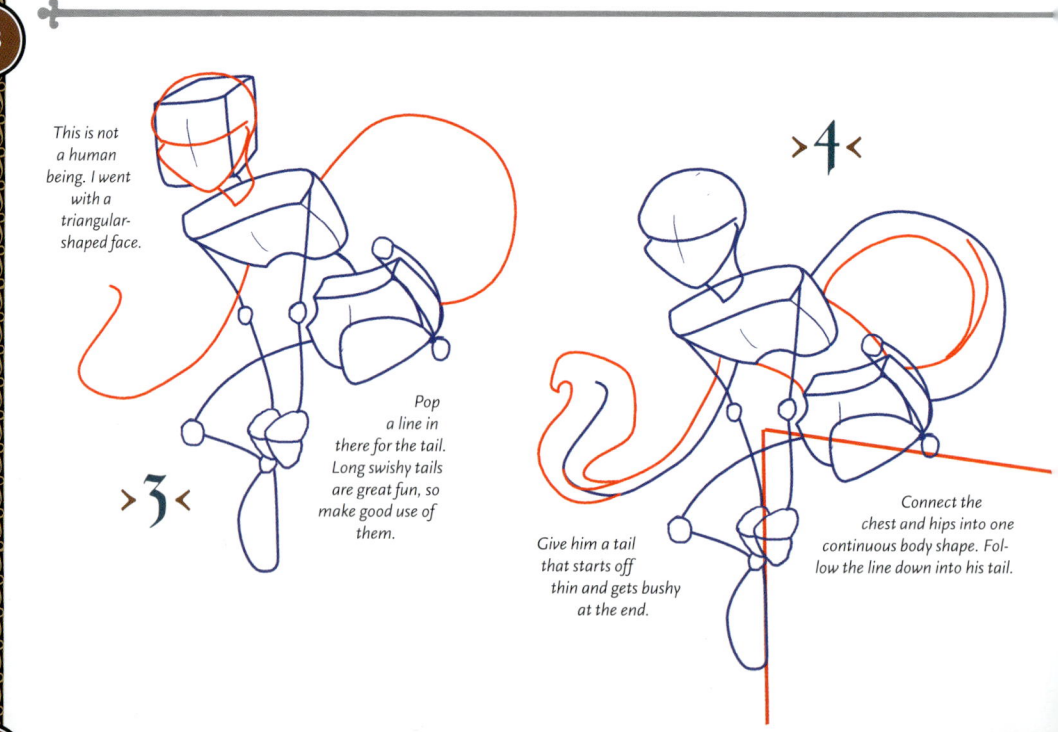

Goblins are fairy-tale creatures of the Unseelie fairy court.

They were notorious for playing pranks and tricks. People would often blame their troubles on them.

Since the idea of goblins and other fairytale creatures is preposterous, I blame all my personal woes on raccoons.

I hate those raccoons...

This is not a human being. I went with a triangular-shaped face.

>3<

Pop a line in there for the tail. Long swishy tails are great fun, so make good use of them.

Give him a tail that starts off thin and gets bushy at the end.

>4<

Connect the chest and hips into one continuous body shape. Follow the line down into his tail.

> 1 <

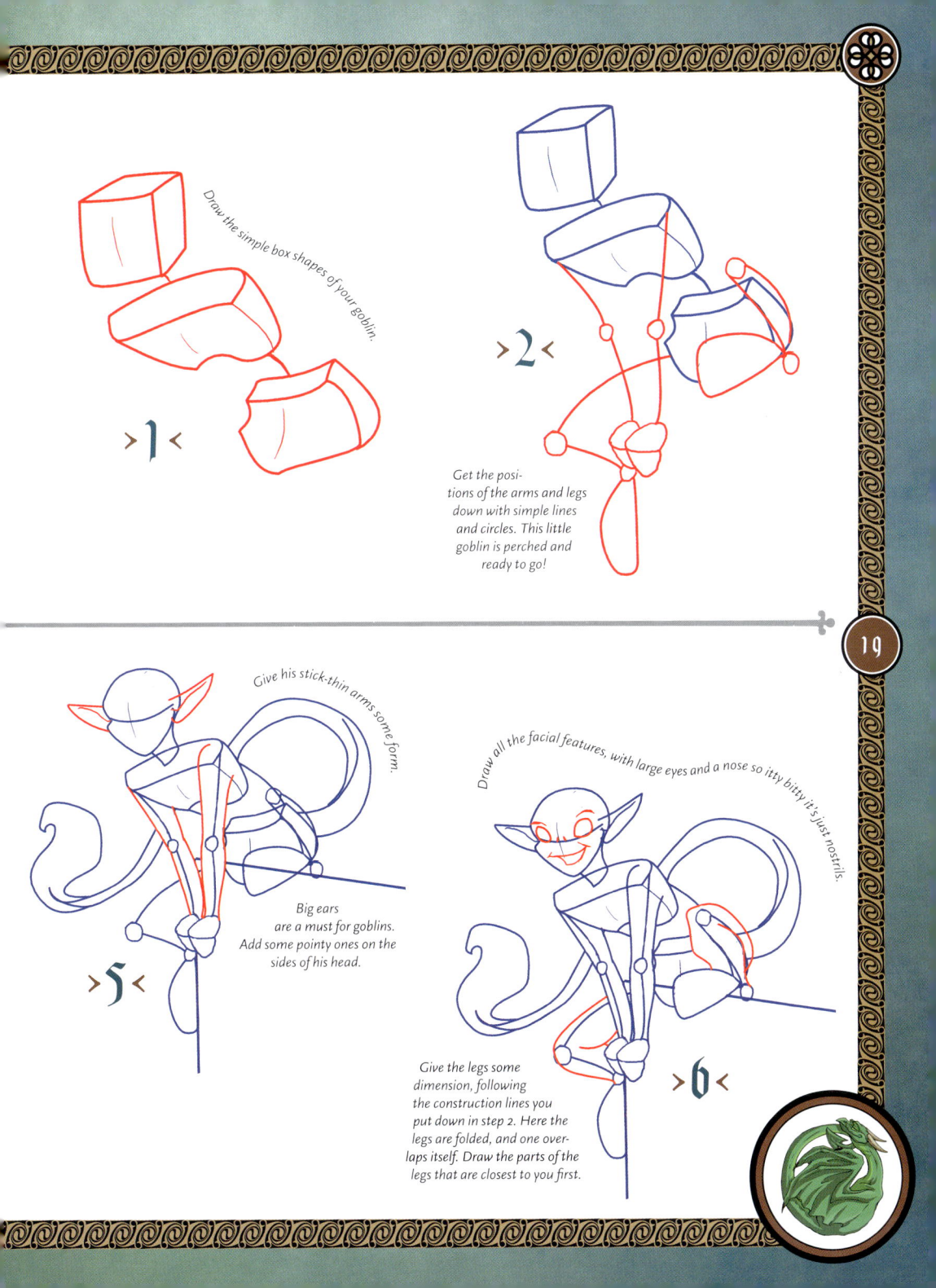

Draw the simple box shapes of your goblin.

> 2 <

Get the positions of the arms and legs down with simple lines and circles. This little goblin is perched and ready to go!

> 5 <

Give his stick-thin arms some form.

Big ears are a must for goblins. Add some pointy ones on the sides of his head.

> 6 <

Draw all the facial features, with large eyes and a nose so itty bitty it's just nostrils.

Give the legs some dimension, following the construction lines you put down in step 2. Here the legs are folded, and one overlaps itself. Draw the parts of the legs that are closest to you first.

19

> 7 <

Elongated, claw-like fingers will make him stand out. Draw in a wild mane of hair, and the basics of your tricky little goblin are complete.

> 8 <

With the construction lines of your goblin down, you'll have a very good idea of what he looks like, so when you get to details like ripples in the clothing, you're good to go!

> 9 <

Once you've got all your details down, erase any extra construction lines. Move onto some scenery. With this drawing, the scenery is particularly important, since the goblin is perching on a corner of some sort. Sketch in the corner of a building that has seen better days.

> 10 <

Color your goblin any color of the rainbow. He can be as bright or as muted as you want. Maybe he's colored like his environment. This goblin is perched in a murky city, so he has muted, murky colors.

21

Dwarf

Dwarves have origins in Norse mythology. Most dwarves are described as being short and stocky with the males (and sometimes the females) sporting long, full beards. Dwarves are fierce, if inelegant, warriors. The stereotypical dwarf is a gruff, grumpy sort who's very set in his ways. Your dwarven character can stick to this cliché, or perhaps yours is just a big softie.

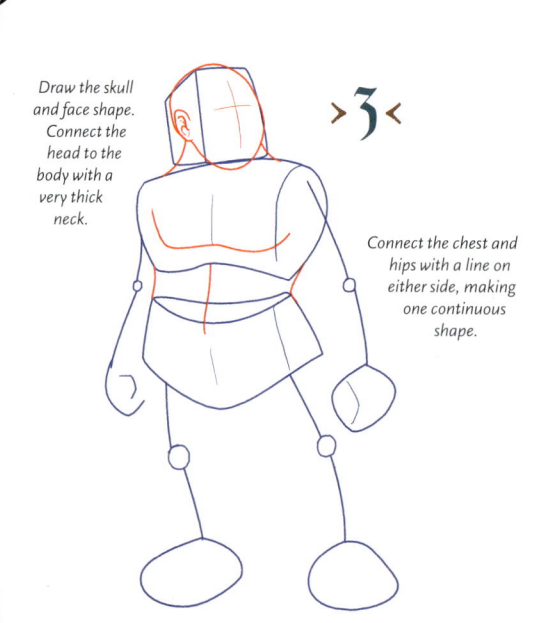

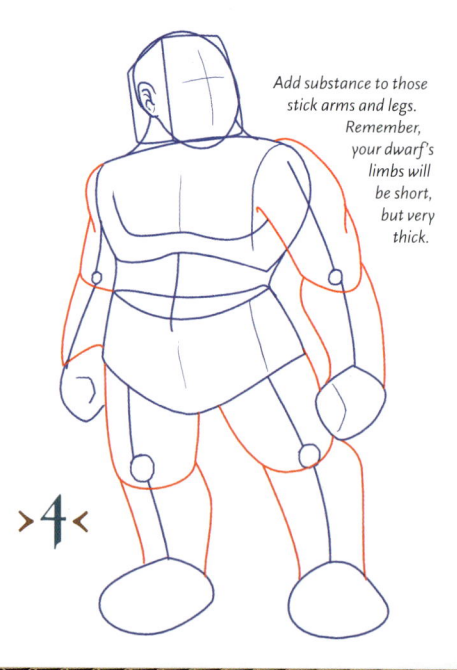

You can tell a lot of different stories with the same character—

—so before you begin—

—carefully consider what you'd like to do with them.

Draw the skull and face shape. Connect the head to the body with a very thick neck.

>3<

Connect the chest and hips with a line on either side, making one continuous shape.

Add substance to those stick arms and legs. Remember, your dwarf's limbs will be short, but very thick.

>4<

> 1 <

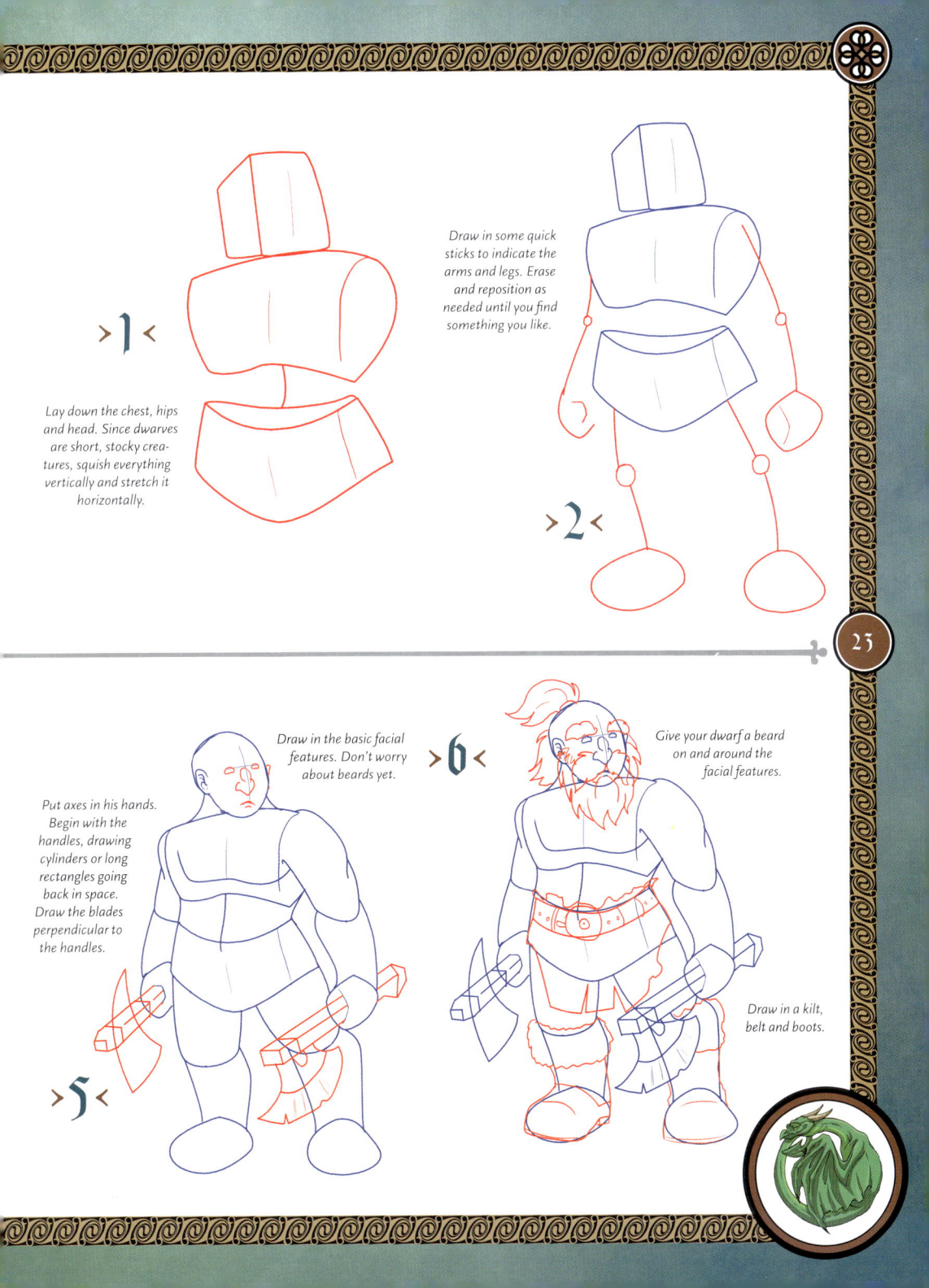

Lay down the chest, hips and head. Since dwarves are short, stocky creatures, squish everything vertically and stretch it horizontally.

Draw in some quick sticks to indicate the arms and legs. Erase and reposition as needed until you find something you like.

> 2 <

23

Put axes in his hands. Begin with the handles, drawing cylinders or long rectangles going back in space. Draw the blades perpendicular to the handles.

Draw in the basic facial features. Don't worry about beards yet.

> 6 <

Give your dwarf a beard on and around the facial features.

Draw in a kilt, belt and boots.

> 5 <

A cape, gloves and shoulder guards finish off the adventurer's look.

>7<

If you like everything you see, begin polishing. Customize belt buckles, goggles and cracks in the armor. Use your pencil in different ways to get different textures. For soft fur, try short rounded marks within and irregular edges. Use hard, perfectly smooth lines for the metallic pieces and watch the magic as the line treatments contrast.

As an added touch, line the gloves and boots with fur.

>8<

Erase any stray construction lines and give yourself a big pat on the back. Oh wait! It's time to color!

>9<

>10<

Typically these gruff warriors won't be prancing around in bright rainbow colors. Their armor may be beautifully constructed, but will probably favor practicality over looks. Your dwarf's beard may be Burnt Sienna, a bright cheery red, a deep black or even an icy blonde in color. Use highlights to add texture. Differentiating the coarseness of the beard, the smoothness of metal, and the fuzziness of fur lining will really make your picture come alive.

25

Centaur

Half man, half horse, in ancient Greek mythology, centaurs were depicted as drunken and rowdy creatures. They were also known for carrying off young maidens. Recent fantasy has taken a different view of centaurs, giving them a more noble character and rational outlook.

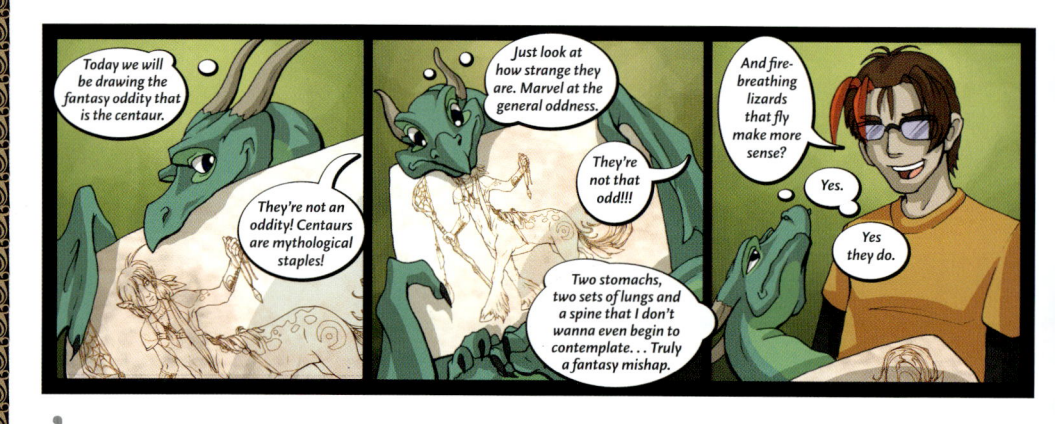

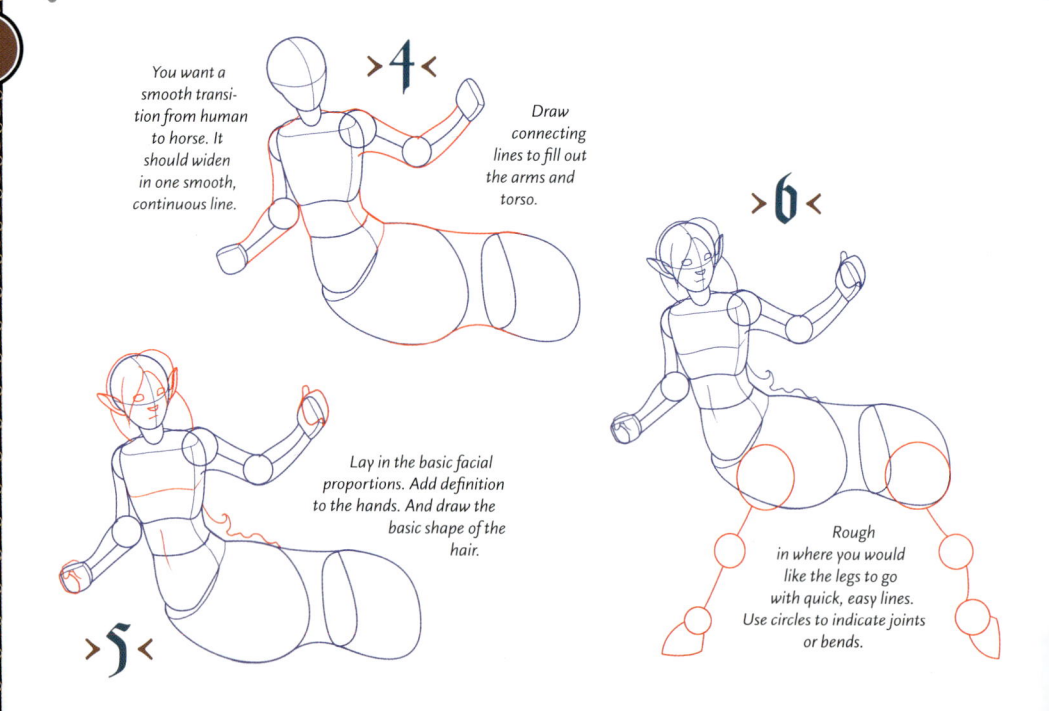

Panel 1: Today we will be drawing the fantasy oddity that is the centaur.
They're not an oddity! Centaurs are mythological staples!

Panel 2: Just look at how strange they are. Marvel at the general oddness.
They're not that odd!!!
Two stomachs, two sets of lungs and a spine that I don't wanna even begin to contemplate... Truly a fantasy mishap.

Panel 3: And fire-breathing lizards that fly make more sense?
Yes.
Yes they do.

> 4 <
Draw connecting lines to fill out the arms and torso.

You want a smooth transition from human to horse. It should widen in one smooth, continuous line.

> 6 <

> 5 <
Lay in the basic facial proportions. Add definition to the hands. And draw the basic shape of the hair.

Rough in where you would like the legs to go with quick, easy lines. Use circles to indicate joints or bends.

> 1 <

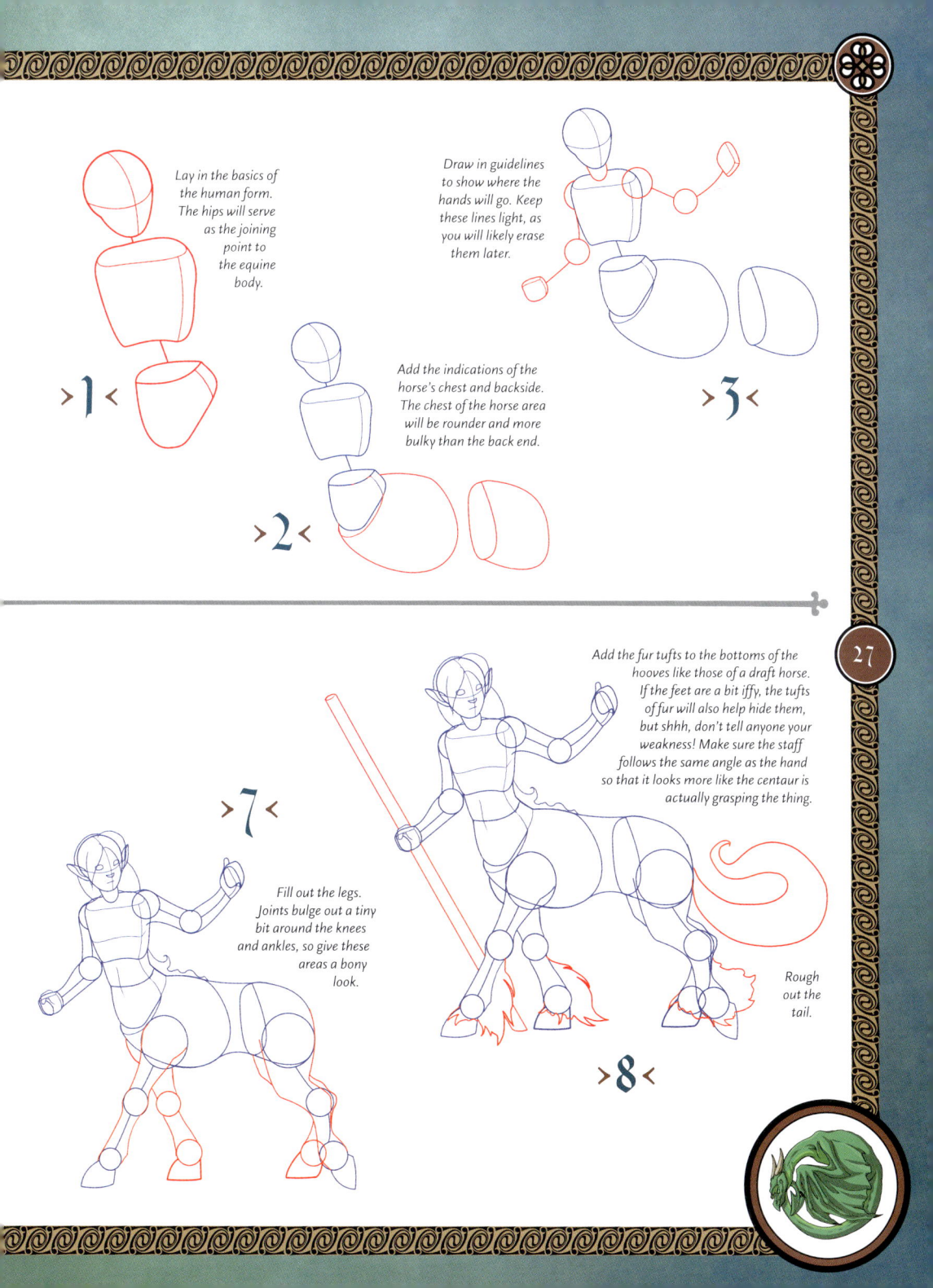

Lay in the basics of the human form. The hips will serve as the joining point to the equine body.

> 2 <

Add the indications of the horse's chest and backside. The chest of the horse area will be rounder and more bulky than the back end.

> 3 <

Draw in guidelines to show where the hands will go. Keep these lines light, as you will likely erase them later.

> 7 <

Fill out the legs. Joints bulge out a tiny bit around the knees and ankles, so give these areas a bony look.

> 8 <

Add the fur tufts to the bottoms of the hooves like those of a draft horse. If the feet are a bit iffy, the tufts of fur will also help hide them, but shhh, don't tell anyone your weakness! Make sure the staff follows the same angle as the hand so that it looks more like the centaur is actually grasping the thing.

Rough out the tail.

> 9 <

Give your centaur some real character, a nifty hairstyle and some unique armor or articles of clothing. Do not get stuck on the face. Work all that love across the entire drawing!

> 10 <

There's a lot of hair and fur on this character; be sure the lines of the hair follow the general shapes you put down earlier. Add spots and patterns to define your centaur. Once you've finished adding detail, clean up any stray construction lines with a soft eraser.

> 11 <

When choosing a color for your centaur, you may want to base it off a particular breed or horse, but you can, of course, make it any color you like!

Carry the "horse" color up the entire length of the creature, so that the definition of where human ends and horse begins is not quite so clear.

>12<

When you're finished with your drawing, carefully consider what sort of setting you'd like your centaur to be in. A mysterious forest, the rolling plains, even an indoor environment could be interesting, and would provide its own challenges. Add as simple or complex of a background as you like. Here, the dim light of the forest casts the majority of the centaurs in shadow.

Sprite

Sprites and spirits are another exciting and visually awesome part of the fairy kingdom. Sprites, like many fairy tale creatures, are mischievous and playful. You may catch a glimpse of one in the water, or hiding behind a leaf, but when you move in for a closer look, you find it's mysteriously disappeared!

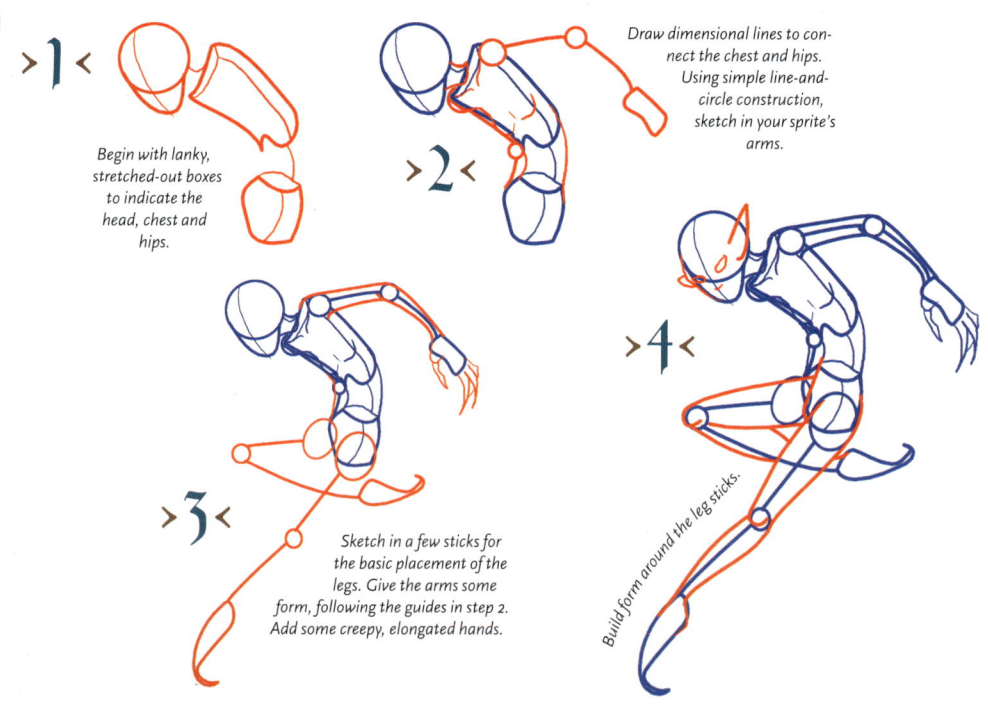

> Backgrounds are very important to any drawing. They give your character a setting, a story. They lend atmosphere and interest.

> Er...you do realize—

> Silence! You're destroying the irony.

> 1 <
Begin with lanky, stretched-out boxes to indicate the head, chest and hips.

> 2 <
Draw dimensional lines to connect the chest and hips. Using simple line-and-circle construction, sketch in your sprite's arms.

> 3 <
Sketch in a few sticks for the basic placement of the legs. Give the arms some form, following the guides in step 2. Add some creepy, elongated hands.

> 4 <
Build form around the leg sticks.

>5<

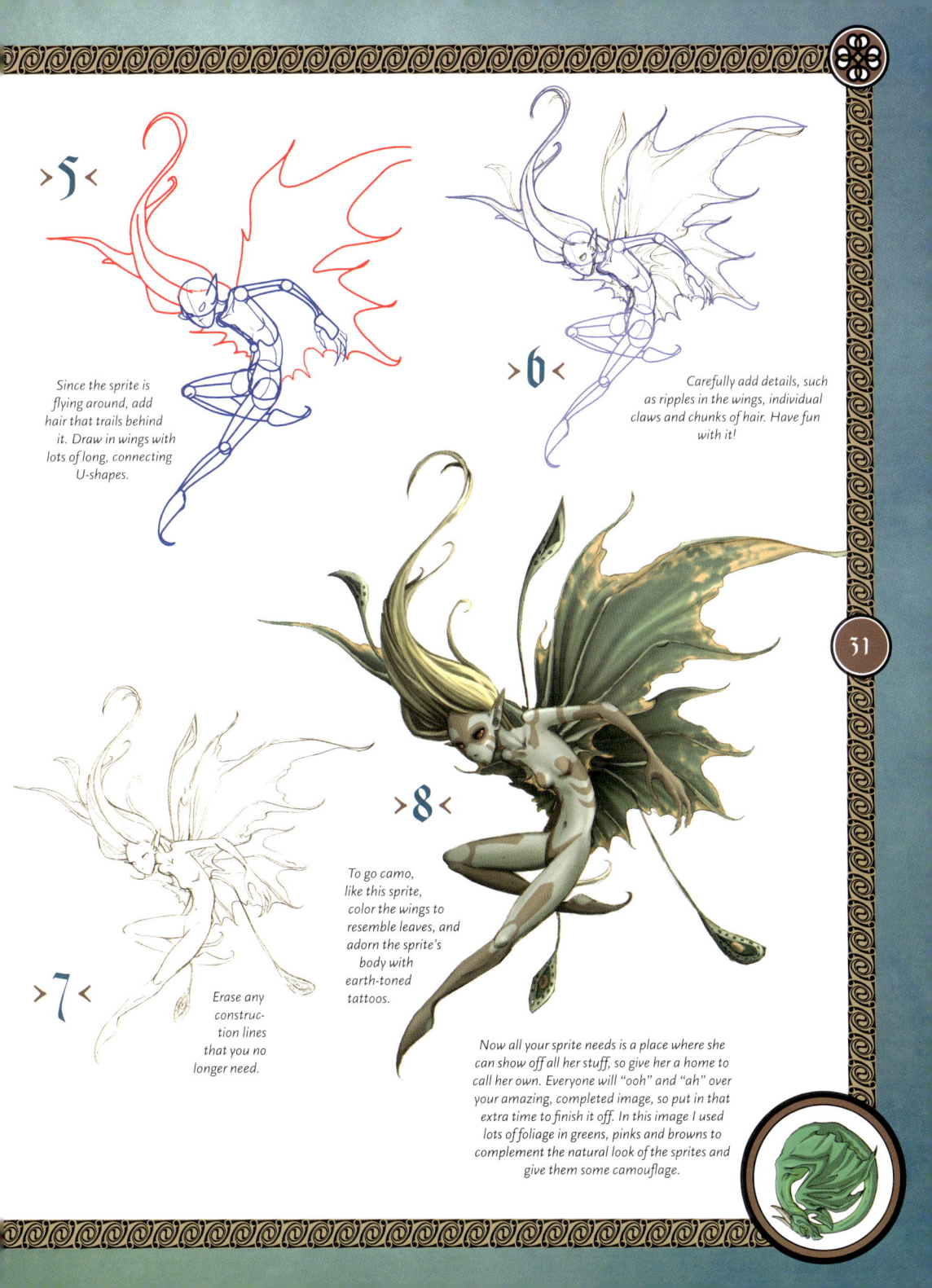

Since the sprite is flying around, add hair that trails behind it. Draw in wings with lots of long, connecting U-shapes.

>6<

Carefully add details, such as ripples in the wings, individual claws and chunks of hair. Have fun with it!

>7<

Erase any construction lines that you no longer need.

>8<

To go camo, like this sprite, color the wings to resemble leaves, and adorn the sprite's body with earth-toned tattoos.

Now all your sprite needs is a place where she can show off all her stuff, so give her a home to call her own. Everyone will "ooh" and "ah" over your amazing, completed image, so put in that extra time to finish it off. In this image I used lots of foliage in greens, pinks and browns to complement the natural look of the sprites and give them some camouflage.

32